IT IS
A GREAT THING
TO SERVE THE LORD

Why You Must Become A Servant of God

Dag Heward-Mills

Parchment House

Unless otherwise stated, all Scripture quotations are taken from the King James Version of the Bible.

IT IS A GREAT THING TO SERVE THE LORD
WHY YOU MUST BECOME A SERVANT OF GOD

Copyright © 2017 Dag Heward-Mills

First published 2017 by Parchment House
3rd Printing 2019

77Find out more about Dag Heward-Mills at:

Healing Jesus Campaign
Email: evangelist@daghewardmills.org
Website: www.daghewardmills.org
Facebook: Dag Heward-Mills
Twitter: @EvangelistDag

ISBN : 978-1-68398-266-1

Contents

CHAPTER 1

Who Is a Servant of God?

Y ou do not have to be a pastor or a missionary to be a servant of God. We all know that priests, prophets, evangelists and pastors are servants of the Lord. We know that such people are privileged to be called the servants of the most high God. What a blessing they have to serve their maker. However, the good news is that other people who are not ministers of the gospel of Jesus Christ can also be servants of God.

Indeed, the bible is full of stories of people who were not pastors but were servants of God. God called them His servants and that is what they were. Some of these men were kings, politicians, businessmen, millionaires, farmers and even non-Jews.

The fact that people, other than priests and evangelists, are called servants of God has great implications for everyone. It means you can be a servant of God! A banker, a lawyer, a doctor, a politician, a pharmacist and a tax collector can be a servant of God.

You do not have to be in full-time ministry to be a servant of God. You can be working in any secular field and still be a servant of God. It is important to take note of all the people God referred to as His "servants".

A servant is somebody who carries out the wishes of another. A servant is someone who serves the interests of another. From now onwards, you must consider yourself a potential servant of God. A student can be a servant of God! A businessman can be a servant of God! A teacher can be a servant of God! You can carry out the wishes of Almighty God no matter your occupation. The greatest job you could ever do is to be a servant of God.

It is no surprise that priests, Levites and prophets are called servants of God. Abraham, Isaac and Jacob were not pastors but God referred to them as His servants. I know that you would like to think of Abraham as a pastor. But Abraham was not a pastor. He was simply a servant of God. I also know that you would consider Moses to be a pastor. However, Moses was the head of state of Israel. God referred to King David as His servant. Indeed, both Moses and David were heads of state of Israel and were predecessors to people like David Ben Gurion, Shimon Peres, Yitzhak Rabin, Ehud Barak, Ariel Sharon and Benjamin Netanyahu. A head of state is not a pastor. A head of state can be a servant of God. Both Moses and David were wonderful servants of God. Make sure that whatever position you occupy, you become a servant of God.

Job was the greatest businessman from the East. Since Job was from the East, he was probably Chinese, Korean or Japanese. Job was so wealthy and yet was called a servant of God. God even boasted to the devil about His servant Job. From heaven's point of view, Job was a servant of God. Today, wealthy businessmen hardly serve the Lord. If you are a businessman, you can be like Job and be a servant of God. This book is being written so that you can become a servant of God. God wants you to be His servant. I would advise you to become God's servant. There are many advantages to being a servant of God. And that is what this book is about! Decide to become a servant of God. Decide that you will be called one of God's servants. Let heaven regard you and respect you as a servant of God. Let us look at the amazing list of people who were called servants of God in the Bible.

1. Priests and Levites were servants of God.

And, behold, the courses of the priests and the Levites, even THEY SHALL BE WITH THEE FOR ALL THE SERVICE OF THE HOUSE OF GOD: and there shall be with thee for all manner of workmanship every willing skilful man, for any manner of service: also the princes and all the people will be wholly at thy commandment.

1 Chronicles 28:21

2. Prophets were servants of God.

And thou shalt smite the house of Ahab thy master, that I may avenge the blood of MY SERVANTS THE PROPHETS, and the blood of all the servants of the Lord, at the hand of Jezebel.

2 Kings 9:7

But my words and my statutes, which I commanded MY SERVANTS THE PROPHETS, did they not take hold of your fathers? and they returned and said, Like as the Lord of hosts thought to do unto us, according to our ways, and according to our doings, so hath he dealt with us.

Zechariah 1:6

3. Abraham, Isaac and Jacob, the greatest businessmen, were all servants of God.

Remember ABRAHAM, ISAAC, AND ISRAEL, THY SERVANTS, to whom thou swarest by thine own self, and saidst unto them, I will multiply your seed as the stars of heaven, and all this land that I have spoken of will I give unto your seed, and they shall inherit it for ever.

Exodus 32:13

3

4.   Jacob, the multimillionaire, was a servant of God.

But thou, ISRAEL, ART MY SERVANT, JACOB WHOM I HAVE CHOSEN, the seed of Abraham my friend. Thou whom I have taken from the ends of the earth, and called thee from the chief men thereof, and said unto thee, Thou art my servant; I have chosen thee, and not cast thee away.

Isaiah 41:8-9

5.   Moses, the head of state, was a servant of God.

Only be thou strong and very courageous, that thou mayest observe to do according to all the law, which MOSES MY SERVANT commanded thee: turn not from it to the right hand or to the left, that thou mayest prosper whithersoever thou goest.

Joshua 1:7

6.   David the king was a servant of God.

And it came to pass, when THE KING sat in his house, and the Lord had given him rest round about from all his enemies; That the king said unto Nathan the prophet, see now, I dwell in an house of cedar, but the ark of God dwelleth within curtains. And Nathan said to the king, Go, do all that is in thine heart; for the Lord is with thee. And it came to pass that night, that the word of the Lord came unto Nathan, saying, GO AND TELL MY SERVANT DAVID, thus saith the Lord, shalt thou build me an house for me to dwell in?

2 Samuel 7:1-5

Therefore now, LORD GOD OF ISRAEL, KEEP WITH THY SERVANT DAVID my father that thou promisedst him, saying, There shall not fail thee a man in my sight to sit on the throne of Israel; so that thy children take heed to their way, that they walk before me as thou hast walked before me. And now, O God of Israel, let thy word, I pray thee, be verified, which thou spakest unto thy servant David my father.

1 Kings 8:25-26

7. **Zerubbabel, a secular governor of Judah and a leader of exiles, was a servant of God.**

In that day, saith the Lord of hosts, will I take thee, O ZERUBBABEL, MY SERVANT, the son of Shealtiel, saith the Lord, and will make thee as a signet: for I have chosen thee, saith the Lord of hosts.

Haggai 2:23

8. **A whole nation was referred to as servants of God. All Israelites were called servants of God and God did not want them to serve another.**

And if thy brother that dwelleth by thee be waxen poor, and be sold unto thee; thou shalt not compel him to serve as a bondservant: But as an hired servant, and as a sojourner, he shall be with thee, and shall serve thee unto the year of jubile: And then shall he depart from thee, both he and his children with him, and shall return unto his own family, and unto the possession of his fathers shall he return. FOR THEY ARE MY SERVANTS, WHICH I BROUGHT FORTH OUT OF THE LAND OF EGYPT: they shall not be sold as bondmen. Thou shalt not rule over him with rigour; but shalt fear thy God.

Leviticus 25:39-43

And as a yearly hired servant shall he be with him: and the other shall not rule with rigour over him in thy sight. And if he be not redeemed in these years, then he shall go out in the year of jubile, both he, and his children with him. For UNTO ME THE CHILDREN OF ISRAEL ARE SERVANTS; they are my servants whom I brought forth out of the land of Egypt: I am the Lord your God.

Leviticus 25:53-55

9. Job, the greatest businessman from the East, was a servant of God.

There was a man in the land of Uz, whose name was Job; and that man was perfect and upright, and one that feared God, and eschewed evil. And there were born unto him seven sons and three daughters. His substance also was seven thousand sheep, and three thousand camels, and five hundred yoke of oxen, and five hundred she asses, and a very great household; so that this man was the greatest of all the men of the east. And his sons went and feasted in their houses, every one his day; and sent and called for their three sisters to eat and to drink with them. And it was so, when the days of their feasting were gone about, that Job sent and sanctified them, and rose up early in the morning, and offered burnt offerings according to the number of them all: for Job said, It may be that my sons have sinned, and cursed God in their hearts. Thus did Job continually. Now there was a day when the sons of God came to present themselves before the Lord, and Satan came also among them. And the Lord said unto Satan, Whence comest thou? Then Satan answered the Lord, and said, from going to and fro in the earth, and from walking up and down in it. And THE LORD SAID UNTO SATAN, HAST THOU CONSIDERED MY SERVANT JOB, that there is none like him in the earth, a perfect and an upright man, one that feareth God, and escheweth evil?

Job 1:1-8

10. Nebuchadnezzar, the Babylonian king, was called the servant of God.

Therefore thus saith the Lord of hosts; Because ye have not heard my words, Behold, I will send and take all the families of the north, saith the Lord, and NEBUCHADREZZAR THE KING OF BABYLON, MY SERVANT, and will bring them against this land, and against the inhabitants thereof, and against all these nations round about, and will utterly destroy them, and make them an astonishment, and an hissing, and perpetual desolations.

Jeremiah 25:8-9

CHAPTER 2

It Is a Great Thing to Serve the Lord: *All Things Shall be Added Unto You*

Therefore I say unto you, Take no thought for your life, what ye shall eat, or what ye shall drink; nor yet for your body, what ye shall put on. Is not the life more than meat, and the body than raiment?

Behold the fowls of the air: for they sow not, neither do they reap, nor gather into barns; yet your heavenly Father feedeth them. Are ye not much better than they?

Which of you by taking thought can add one cubit unto his stature?

And why take ye thought for raiment? Consider the lilies of the field, how they grow; they toil not, neither do they spin:

And yet I say unto you, That even Solomon in all his glory was not arrayed like one of these.

Wherefore, if God so clothe the grass of the field, which to day is, and to morrow is cast into the oven, shall he not much more clothe you, O ye of little faith?

Therefore take no thought, saying, What shall we eat? or, What shall we drink? or, Wherewithal shall we be clothed?

(For after all these things do the Gentiles seek:) for your heavenly Father knoweth that ye have need of all these things

But seek ye first the kingdom of God, and his righteousness; and all these things shall be added unto you.

Matthew 6:25-33

1. SEEKING THE LORD FIRST IS THE MASTER KEY IN MATTHEW 6:33. INDEED, IT IS YOUR MASTER KEY TO PROSPERITY.

Being a servant of someone is to seek and serve his interests and not your own. Seeking God's kingdom and God's righteousness is the same as serving God. You must seek to become a servant of God. Therefore you must seek the kingdom of God and His righteousness. As we have already learnt, it is possible for anyone to become a servant of God. It is possible for anyone in any profession to be a servant of God. It is important to seek that status – the status of being God's servant. Becoming God's servant is far more important than becoming a doctor or a lawyer.

To serve someone is to seek his interests. To serve God is to seek God's interests. To seek God's interests is to seek His kingdom and His righteousness.

To serve someone is to contribute to and promote the person. To serve God is to contribute to God's work and to promote God's kingdom in your life.

To serve someone is to be useful or of service to him. To serve God is to be useful or of service to Him.

To serve someone is to be obedient to his wishes. To serve God is to be obedient to his wishes!

It is important to seek to be a servant of God. Most people do not know or understand why seeking God first is so important. Seeking God is the most profitable activity you can ever engage in. Seeking God is the one thing that will cause all other things to be added to your life. All other things that people are dying for are simply added to your life when you seek the Lord.

Matthew 6:33 is the master secret to your prosperity in this life! The secret to all things that people are seeking for is to seek God first. As you seek the Lord, everything else will be added to your life.

When you truly serve God, eating, drinking and clothing will be the easiest things for you to acquire. God gives all things that men seek for to those who seek His kingdom first. What you shall eat, what you shall drink and what you shall wear shall no longer be something to think about in this life. It is taken care of by seeking God first.

Matthew 6:33 is unlocked by letting your mind be on God's work and not on your own work. The key to receiving the wages of God, is to let your mind be on God's work and not on your own work. "Take no thought for your own life"! This is a direct instruction from God. Yet most Christians simply take thoughts for their own lives.

Jesus said, "Come unto me, all ye that labour and are heavy laden, and I will give you rest. Take my yoke upon you, and learn of me; for I am meek and lowly in heart: and ye shall find rest unto your souls. For my yoke is easy, and my burden is light" (Matthew 11:28-30).

You have to give Him your yoke, the burden of your life and the burden of your work. Then, you have to take up His burden and His work. That is the secret to the prosperity hidden in Matthew 6:33. Seeking the kingdom of God means, "Do not seek your own kingdom." Once you set about to seek your own kingdom, you have broken the law of Matthew 6:33.

Through the secret in Matthew 6:33, you will have a house to live in and a car to drive. When you follow the prosperity key hidden within Matthew 6:33, you will never have to take a thought for your own life. To eat, to drink and to dress up will be taken care of. This means you will have money to buy food, a place to cook it and a car to go and get your clothes. Matthew 6:33 is a very wide-ranging scripture with wide-ranging implications.

To fully trust in the promise of Matthew 6:33 is to become like the lilies of the field which were more prosperous than even

Solomon. Through the secret of Matthew 6:33, your prosperity will eventually be compared to the prosperity of Solomon. God can clothe you better, feed you better and care for you far better than you can do for yourself.

2. SEEKING THE LORD FIRST WAS THE MASTER KEY TO KING UZZIAH. INDEED, IT WAS HIS MASTER KEY TO PROSPERITY.

Uzziah (also called Azariah) is famously mentioned by the prophet Isaiah when he said "In the year king Uzziah died, I saw the Lord." Isaiah was called in the very year that King Uzziah died. Uzziah came to the throne when he was only sixteen years old and reigned prosperously for fifty-two years. He was one of the most outstanding kings because of the things he achieved. He is one of the few kings who lived that long and prospered so much. He invented weapons, strengthened himself and was able to build even in the desert.

Zechariah, the prophet urged the king to seek the Lord. As he sought the Lord, King Uzziah prospered and became very strong. You may wonder what is the connection between seeking God and "prospering". Indeed, there is a great connection. The bible is plain. You cannot add to the truth! You cannot subtract from the truth! You can only accept the truth!

a. As long as King Uzziah sought the Lord he prospered.

Sixteen years old was Uzziah when he began to reign, and he reigned fifty and two years in Jerusalem. His mother's name also was Jecoliah of Jerusalem. And he did that which was right in the sight of the Lord, according to all that his father Amaziah did. AND HE SOUGHT GOD IN THE DAYS OF ZECHARIAH, who had understanding in the visions of God: and AS LONG AS HE SOUGHT THE LORD, GOD MADE HIM TO PROSPER.

2 Chronicles 26:3-5

b. As King Uzziah sought the Lord, people gave gifts to him.

And THE AMMONITES GAVE GIFTS TO UZZIAH: and his name spread abroad even to the entering in of Egypt; for he strengthened himself exceedingly.

2 Chronicles 26:8

c. As King Uzziah sought the Lord, his name spread abroad.

And the Ammonites gave gifts to Uzziah: and HIS NAME SPREAD ABROAD even to the entering in of Egypt; for he strengthened himself exceedingly.

2 Chronicles 26:8

d. As King Uzziah sought the Lord, he strengthened himself.

And the Ammonites gave gifts to Uzziah: and his name spread abroad even to the entering in of Egypt; for HE STRENGTHENED HIMSELF exceedingly.

2 Chronicles 26:8

e. As King Uzziah sought the Lord, he built towers in the desert.

Moreover Uzziah built towers in Jerusalem at the corner gate, and at the valley gate, and at the turning of the wall, and fortified them. Also HE BUILT TOWERS IN THE DESERT, and digged many wells: for he had much cattle, both in the low country, and in the plains: husbandmen also, and vine dressers in the mountains, and in Carmel: for he loved husbandry.

2 Chronicles 26:9-10

f.   As King Uzziah sought the Lord, he had a host of fighting men.

Moreover UZZIAH HAD AN HOST OF FIGHTING MEN, that went out to war by bands, according to the number of their account by the hand of Jeiel the scribe and Maaseiah the ruler, under the hand of Hananiah, one of the king's captains. The whole number of the chief of the fathers of the mighty men of valour were two thousand and six hundred. And under their hand was an army, three hundred thousand and seven thousand and five hundred, that made war with mighty power, to help the king against the enemy.

2 Chronicles 26:11-13

g.   As King Uzziah sought the Lord, he made engines invented by cunning men. Seeking the Lord made him wise.

And HE MADE in Jerusalem ENGINES, INVENTED BY CUNNING MEN, to be on the towers and upon the bulwarks, to shoot arrows and great stones withal. And his name spread far abroad; for he was marvellously helped, till he was strong.

2 Chronicles 26:15

h.   As King Uzziah sought the Lord, he was marvellously helped.

And he made in Jerusalem engines, invented by cunning men, to be on the towers and upon the bulwarks, to shoot arrows and great stones withal. And his name spread far abroad; for HE WAS MARVELLOUSLY HELPED, till he was strong.

2 Chronicles 26:15

3. **SEEKING THE LORD FIRST WAS THE MASTER KEY FOR KING DAVID. INDEED, IT WAS HIS MASTER KEY TO NOT NEEDING ANYTHING.**

It is a great thing to serve the Lord because when you are a servant of God, you will be blessed with every good thing.

O taste and see that the Lord is good: blessed is the man that trusteth in him. O fear the Lord, ye his saints: for there is no want to them that fear him. The young lions do lack, and suffer hunger: but THEY THAT SEEK THE LORD SHALL NOT WANT ANY GOOD THING.

Psalm 34:8-10

Your wages for seeking the Lord and doing His work know no limits. This amazing scripture now adds "every good thing" to the long list of things you can expect to receive from the Lord as you serve Him. Truly, prosperity is one of the greatest mysteries of our world today. No one really knows what makes one person prosper and the other turn into nothing.

4. **SEEKING THE LORD FIRST IS THE MASTER KEY TO GREAT REWARDS.**

... he that cometh to God must believe that he is, and that he is a REWARDER of them that diligently SEEK HIM.

Hebrews 11:6

The principle is the same and the scriptures are saying the same thing. Seeking God is a master key to great rewards. Seeking God and becoming a servant of God is the key you have been looking for.

It is a great thing to serve the Lord because when you are a servant of God, He will reward you. Instead of seeking jobs with mere men, seek to be a servant of God. Your job with God is more important than your job with men.

Expect great rewards for seeking God. God is a God who rewards!

Expect a reward of God's blessings as you seek Him. God is a God who blesses!

Expect a reward of great protection for seeking God. God is a God who protects!

Expect a reward of great prosperity as you seek God. God is a God who makes you prosper!

Expect a reward of peace as you seek God. God is a God who gives peace!

Expect a reward of multiplication as you seek God. God is a God who multiplies things under your hands!

Expect a reward of great miracles as you seek God. God is a God who does miracles!

Expect a reward of healing as you seek God. God is a God who heals!

Expect a reward of great deliverance as you seek God. God is a God who delivers!

Expect a supply of your needs.

Expect a reward of pleasures forever more.

Expect a reward of abundance.

Expect God to make you shine in this life and in eternity.

God actually wants you to see Him as a rewarder. Expect a river of rewards and nothing else! Expect to be blessed as you serve God. Walk forward and fulfil your ministry, expecting God to reward you for being His servant.

Most people think that there is something wrong in expecting rewards from God, but God's word teaches us to expect rewards. God actually loves it when we expect good rewards for serving Him. We are quicker to believe that God is a punisher of people who make mistakes. God likes it when people think nice things about Him.

5. SEEKING THE LORD FIRST WILL NEVER BE IN VAIN.

I have not spoken in secret, in a dark place of the earth: I SAID NOT UNTO THE SEED OF JACOB, SEEK YE ME IN VAIN: I the Lord speak righteousness, I declare things that are right.

Isaiah 45:19

It is a great thing to serve the Lord because you will never seek God in vain.

The seed of Jacob will not serve in vain. God is a righteous God. No one serves God in vain. To serve in vain is to waste your time. To serve in vain is to do an activity that is to no purpose. To serve in vain is to serve without having and seeing the desired outcome.

Do not think of God in a bad way. Do not think of Him as someone who will leave you penniless at the end of all your hard work.

You will not serve God in vain! To serve in vain is to engage in a fruitless, worthless and useless activity. Serving God cannot and will never be a fruitless, worthless and useless activity! You will be glad you served the Lord. He has not asked the seed of Jacob to serve Him in vain.

CHAPTER 3

It is a Great Thing to Serve the Lord: *You Will Receive Good Wages*

And HE THAT REAPETH RECEIVETH WAGES, and gathereth fruit unto life eternal: that both he that soweth and he that reapeth may rejoice together.

John 4:36

Awage is something that comes to you because of the work or service you have done. Wages can be given to you on a daily, weekly or monthly basis. Since God gives wages, you can expect blessings of wages on a daily, weekly, monthly or yearly basis.

Wages are therefore incomes, earnings, returns, salaries, compensation, payments, pay-offs, remuneration, emoluments, reimbursements, allowances, fees, honorariums, awards, advances, rewards, benefits, stipends, remittances and pensions.

These different words reveal the different kinds of wages you can expect to receive for serving God. Expect wages from God as you serve Him. God will pay you for the work you do for Him. Let us look at the different kinds of wages a servant of God should expect.

Twenty Types of Wages You Can Expect

1. *Incomes* are a type of wages. Expect incomes from God as you serve Him. *An income is the money comes into your pocket for the work you have done.* You must therefore expect a good income to be paid to you as you serve God. These incomes are the wages you can expect from God as you reap the harvest of souls.

2. *Earnings* are a type of wages. Expect earnings from God as you serve Him. *An earning is a sum of money you get by working.* You must therefore expect amounts of money to be paid to you as you serve God. These earnings are the wages you can expect from God as you reap the harvest of souls.

3. *Returns* are a type of wages. Expect returns from God as you serve Him. *A return is the gain you realize for the work you have done.* You must therefore expect a good return as you serve God. These returns are the wages you can expect from God as you reap the harvest of souls.

4. *Salaries* are a type of wages. Expect salaries from God as you serve Him. *A salary is the money that someone is paid each month by his employer.* Since you have been employed by God, you can expect a good salary from heaven. These salaries are the wages you can expect from God as you serve in the house of God.

5. *Compensation* is a type of wage. Expect compensations from God as you serve Him. *A compensation is money that is given to someone who has experienced loss or suffering.* You will be paid for whatever you have lost and whatever you have suffered. You must therefore expect a good compensation to be paid to you as you serve God. These compensations are the wages you can expect from God as you stay in His service.

6. *Payments* are a type of wages. Expect payments from God as you serve Him. *A payment is the money you earn for the work you have done.* You must therefore expect a good payment to be paid to you as you serve God. These payments are the wages you can expect from God as you reap the harvest of souls.

7. *Pay-offs* are a type of wages. Expect incomes from God as you serve Him. *A pay-off is a large amount paid to someone by their employer when the person is forced to leave their job.* When you come into full time ministry, you are forced to leave your secular employment. I had to leave my medical profession in order to work for God full-time. You can expect large amounts to be paid to you by God because you had to leave your job.

8. *Remunerations* are a type of wages. Expect remunerations from God as you serve Him. *A remuneration is the act of paying for goods and services and to recompense losses.* Rest assured that whatever goods and services you have provided for Jesus and whatever losses you have made will be paid for. You must therefore expect a good remuneration to be paid to you as you serve God. These

remunerations are the wages you can expect from God as you serve in the house of God.

9.   *Emoluments* are a type of wages. Expect emoluments from God as you serve Him. *An emolument is an alternative form of payment that a person receives for doing work.* You will be paid in kind, you will be given gifts, you will be given privileges which are all a part of your wages given to you by God. These emoluments are the wages you can expect from God as you serve in the house of God.

10.   *Reimbursements* are a type of wages. Expect reimbursements from God as you serve Him. *A reimbursement is the compensation paid for damages and losses.* You must therefore expect a good reimbursement to be paid to you for all the things you have done in the service of the King. Think of all the money you have spent visiting people, following-up people, going to church and working for God. You will surely be reimbursed by the angels of the Lord. These reimbursements are the wages you can expect from God as you serve in the house of God.

11.   *Allowances* are a type of wages. Expect allowances from God as you serve Him. *An allowance is the sum of money given to someone for some personal or general expenses.* Allowances are usually given when a real salary is not available. You can expect wonderful allowances to be paid to you as you serve God. These allowances are the wages you can expect from God Himself.

12.   *Fees* are also a type of wages. Expect fees from God as you serve Him. *A fee is a fixed charge for professional services.* You may have to pay school fees for your children. You may also have to pay a doctor's fee. Think of the school fees that you have to pay so that a teacher teaches your children. Imagine the kind of fees you must

be paid for teaching the word of God. Consider that the word of God is far more important than Chemistry or Biology. You will receive fees from heaven above.

13. *Honorariums* are a type of wages. Expect honorariums from God as you serve Him. *An honorarium is an amount of money given to a speaker for honouring a speaking engagement.* God has huge honorariums stacked up for you for the various speaking engagements you have honoured in His name. The times you have spoken the word of God and honoured Jesus will never be forgotten in heaven. These honorariums are the wages you can expect from God as you serve in the house of God. You must expect a good honorarium to be paid to you as you serve God.

14. *Awards* are also a type of wages. Expect awards from God as you serve Him. *An award is a prize or a certificate that a person is given for doing something well.* There are many prizes and certificates lined up for you as you serve the Lord.

15. *Advances* are a type of wages. *An advance is an amount of money that is paid to someone ahead of time.* An advance is something that is given to you even before you work. You can expect God to load you with benefits even before you start serving Him. He knows your heart and He knows those who will actually serve Him. Advances are very common as you serve the Lord.

16. *Rewards* are a type of wages. Expect rewards from God as you serve Him. *A reward is something that is given to someone because he had behaved well, worked hard or provided a service.* You can expect great rewards for your good behaviour in the house of God. Rewards are the wages you can expect from God as you serve Him.

17. *Benefits* are a type of wages. Expect benefits from God as you serve Him. *A benefit is a non-monetary kind of payment that is given by an employer.* There are many non-monetary payments you can expect as you serve the Lord. Privileges, respect, honour, kindness, gifts, good treatment, kingly treatment, are some of the few benefits that you can expect in the house of God.

18. *Stipends* are a type of wages. Expect a stipend from God as you serve Him. *A stipend is a sum of money granted to a student for his living expenses.* Even as you are a student preacher, learning to be a pastor, you can expect stipends from heaven above. Do not be worried because you are a student in the house of God. God honours His students. Even when you are in school you can expect wages from heaven above.

19. *Remittances* are a type of wages. Expect remittances from God as you serve Him. *A remittance is the money that is sent to a person in another town.* You can expect several remittances to hit your account as you serve the Lord. Even though heaven is far away from earth, arrangements are being made all the time to send money to you on this earth because you serve the Lord.

20. *Pensions* are a type of wages. Expect pensions from God as you serve Him. *A pension is a regular amount paid to you for services you rendered in the past or because you have retired from active service.* You will receive money from God long after you retire from His work.

   "He that reapeth receiveth wages". You will receive the wages of reaping the souls and the harvest that God has ordained for us. The wages for reaping the harvest are the master key to prosperity, success and God's blessing.

CHAPTER 4

It is a Great Thing to Serve the Lord:
There Will be a Difference Between Those who Serve the Lord And Those Who Serve Him Not

And they shall be mine, saith the Lord of hosts, in that day when I make up my jewels; and I WILL SPARE THEM, as a man spareth his own son that serveth him. Then shall ye return, and DISCERN BETWEEN THE RIGHTEOUS AND THE WICKED, between him that serveth God and him that serveth him not.

Malachi 3:17-18

Malachi is famous for his warnings on not tithing. But I think there is an even more serious warning from Malachi for us all. Please take note of Malachi's warning to those who do not serve the Lord: God will cause a big difference to arise between those who serve and those who do not serve.

There will always be a difference between those who serve the Lord and those who do not serve the Lord. Jesus told us about a certain man who had two sons. One of the sons chose to serve in the house and the other chose to leave. One decided that it was a good idea to be a servant in his father's house and work humbly in the fields. Today, we can choose to work humbly in our Father's harvest fields or we can choose to go out on a frolic of our own. We can choose to follow fantasies and the worldly ideas of men. I choose to be a servant of the Lord and work in His field. The promise is clear! You will return and see a difference between those who serve the Lord and those who serve Him not!

The story of the prodigal son is the best example of this principle. In the end, there was a big difference between the one who served in the house and the one who decided not to serve in the father's house. Please notice the stark differences that arise between those who serve the Lord and those who do not serve Him.

Malachi is not the only prophet who warns about the difference that will arise between those who serve and those who do not serve. The prophet Isaiah also warns us that serious differences will arise between those who serve God and those who do not.

Therefore will I number you to the sword, and ye shall all bow down to the slaughter: because when I called, ye did not answer; when I spake, ye did not hear; but did evil before mine eyes, and did choose that wherein I delighted not.

Therefore thus saith the Lord God, BEHOLD, MY SERVANTS SHALL EAT, BUT YE SHALL BE

HUNGRY: BEHOLD, MY SERVANTS SHALL DRINK, BUT YE SHALL BE THIRSTY: BEHOLD, MY SERVANTS SHALL REJOICE, BUT YE SHALL BE ASHAMED:

BEHOLD, MY SERVANTS SHALL SING FOR JOY OF HEART, BUT YE SHALL CRY FOR SORROW OF HEART, AND SHALL HOWL FOR VEXATION OF SPIRIT.

Isaiah 65:12-14

Seven Differences between Those Who Serve And Those Who Do Not Serve

1. As you serve God, there will be a difference between your status and the status of those who do not serve God. The prodigal son was lowered to the rank of a servant. When he came back home, he asked permission to be put at the level of a servant. Indeed, he had lost everything and was not any higher than a servant. His status was completely different from his brother's. His brother was a joint heir with his father. He was a mere servant with no rights, no money, no property and no good standing.

    And the son said unto him, Father, I have sinned against heaven, and in thy sight, and am NO MORE WORTHY TO BE CALLED THY SON.

    Luke 15:21

2. When you serve God, there will be a difference in the covering over your life. The prodigal son was in great need and no one gave him help. When you have a covering you will always receive help from your father and from the cover that is over your defenceless head. Everyone is going to need help at some point in time. Woe to you if you lose the covering over your defenceless head!

And he went and joined himself to a citizen of that country; and he sent him into his fields to feed swine.

Luke 15:15

3. When you serve God, there will be a difference in the outcomes of your life. The prodigal son had become a beggar by the time he learnt his lesson of not serving in the house of his father. Please do not become a beggar by not serving the Lord. I have seen many people lose all that they had by chasing fantasies. Serving the Lord is the most important activity you can ever engage in.

And when he came to himself, he said, How many hired servants of my father's have bread enough and to spare, and I PERISH WITH HUNGER!

Luke 15:17

4. When you serve God, there will be a difference in the peace you enjoy. The prodigal son had no peace in the far away land that he had chosen for himself. Even the pigs were quarrelling with him over the food that he was to eat. Nobody wanted to know him any more. He was no longer an important person. No one helped him and no one liked him! On the other hand, the older brother was riding high as the only remaining heir to his father's estate.

And he went and joined himself to a citizen of that country; and he sent him into his fields to feed swine. And HE WOULD FAIN HAVE FILLED HIS BELLY WITH THE HUSKS THAT THE SWINE DID EAT: and no man gave unto him.

Luke 15:15-16

O that thou hadst hearkened to my commandments! THEN HAD THY PEACE BEEN AS A RIVER, and thy righteousness as the waves of the sea: Thy seed also had been as the sand, and the offspring of thy bowels

like the gravel thereof; his name should not have been cut off nor destroyed from before me.

Isaiah 48:18-19

5.   When you serve God, there will be a difference in your prosperity level. The prodigal son had nothing to his name. His father told the elder brother, the humble servant; "all that I have is yours." The younger brother, who had refused to serve, was basically reduced to the clothes he was wearing. Remember that the clothes he was wearing were gifts he had received on arrival.

And he answering said to his father, Lo, THESE MANY YEARS DO I SERVE THEE, neither transgressed I at any time thy commandment: and yet thou never gavest me a kid, that I might make merry with my friends:... And he said unto him, Son, thou art ever with me, and ALL THAT I HAVE IS THINE.

Luke 15:29, 31

6.   When you serve God, there will be a difference in how your father relates with you. When you are a good servant of God, your father will tell you his secrets and share his powerful revelations with you. The prodigal son was welcomed and given a party, but the older brother who had been a faithful servant was told the truth. His father told him secretly, "All that I have is thine because you are always with me." To the young prodigal son, he just said, "Welcome home."

And he said unto him, Son, thou art ever with me, and all that I have is thine.

Luke 15:31

7.   As you serve God, there will be an absolute difference between those who serve and those who do not serve. The father spoke about his son who had resisted the idea of being a servant in the house. He said, "My son was

lost." He also said, "My son was dead." In other words when you are not a servant in the house of the Lord you are dead. When you are not a servant in the house of the Lord, you are lost. Wow! When you are a servant in the house, you are found! When you are a servant in the house you are alive! Indeed, there is a difference between those that serve the Lord and those that serve Him not!

It was meet that we should make merry, and be glad: for this thy brother was dead, and is alive again; and was lost, and is found.

Luke 15:32

CHAPTER 5

It is a Great Thing to Serve the Lord: *You Will Have Divine Protection*

1. **It is a great thing to serve the Lord because when you are a servant of God, He will mark you and protect you.**

    And after these things I saw four angels standing on the four corners of the earth, holding the four winds of the earth, that the wind should not blow on the earth, nor on the sea, nor on any tree.

    And I saw another angel ascending from the east, having the seal of the living God: and he cried with a loud voice to the four angels, to whom it was given to hurt the earth and the sea, saying, HURT NOT THE EARTH, NEITHER THE SEA, NOR THE TREES, TILL WE HAVE SEALED THE SERVANTS OF OUR GOD in their foreheads.

    Revelation 7:1-3

    As you can see from this powerful scripture, the angel of the Lord marked the servants of the Lord. A great destruction was determined on the earth but the angel of the Lord sealed the servants of God. These servants were counted worthy to escape the destruction that was determined.

The prophet declared, "Since you are precious in my sight, I have loved thee and will give men in exchange for your life" (Isaiah 43:4). God will grant you divine escapes from many evils because He is preserving you. You must always remember that you are precious in the sight of God because you have become His servant.

Perhaps, if you were not a servant of the Lord, you would have died a long time ago. Perhaps you cannot see the invisible mark that is upon your head because you are His servant. Indeed, there is an invisible mark on you. God has marked you and the mark is visible to angels. All God's servants are marked and sealed! It is because of this mark that you are not destroyed. God is protecting you every day because you are His servant.

2.   **It is a great thing to serve the Lord because when you are a servant of God, He will loose you out of your bondages.**

O LORD, TRULY I AM THY SERVANT; I AM THY SERVANT, AND THE SON OF THINE HANDMAID: THOU HAST LOOSED MY BONDS. I will offer to thee the sacrifice of thanksgiving, and will call upon the name of the Lord. I will pay my vows unto the Lord now in the presence of all his people, in the courts of the Lord's house, in the midst of thee, O Jerusalem. Praise ye the Lord.

Psalms 116:16-19

God has great compassion for His servants. He will loose your bands and loose your bonds. God is the kindest boss any one could ever have. He cares so much for His servants. There are some bosses who really love the people who work for them. They may not be biologically related to them but they seem to adopt them as their own children.

One day, a man sent messengers to see Jesus. This man was a centurion, a commander of at least a hundred soldiers. He had a special request to make to Jesus. His servant was sick and needed healing desperately. It is this man who said, "I have men under me and I say to one, 'Go' and he goeth and to another 'Come' and he cometh."

Jesus was touched by the man's faith and healed the centurion's servant. You will notice that it was not the centurion's son or daughter who was sick, but his servant. Indeed, even the wicked Roman soldiers had feelings for their servants. God has great feelings for you, His servant! He will loose your bands and set you free because He is your loving Master. It is a great thing to serve the Lord. It is a great thing to serve such a kind person.

3.   It is a great thing to serve the Lord because when you are a servant of God, He will cut off your enemies.

And of thy mercy CUT OFF MINE ENEMIES, and destroy all them that afflict my soul: FOR I AM THY SERVANT.

Psalms 143:12

God will cut off your enemies. It is not possible to come to this life without having enemies. Out of His mercy for His servant, He will cut off your enemies so that you do not see them any more. When your enemies are cut off, you do not see them anymore, you do not interact with them any more. God will silence all enemies in your life just because you are His servant.

Daniel was taken into the lion's den. He was served as dinner to the lions. The hungry lions looked at their dinner and simply lost their appetite. This miracle was recorded for your encouragement. Whatever represents a lion in your life will be cut off from today! The king was forced to put Daniel in the lion's den but he desperately wanted Daniel to escape. Early in the morning he rushed to the mouth of the lions' den and shouted out, "O Daniel, servant of the living God, is thy God, whom thou servest continually, able to deliver thee from the lions?" But God had sent His angels to deliver Daniel because he was a servant of God.

Whoever stands as an enemy to your life will be cut off because you are a servant of God! In the end, all the accusers of Daniel were thrown into the lions' den. The king commanded that they be disposed of in the same lions' den. This time, the lions wasted no time in eating up the people who were dropped to the bottom of the pit. They crushed their bones, ate their flesh, their livers, their kidneys, their skulls and every part of their bodies. This shows that the lions were indeed hungry and capable of killing and eating anyone. These were really hungry lions that had been tempted with Daniel's meat the night before but were restrained by angels. All the accusers of Daniel, their wives and their children, were eaten up by the lions! How come the lions ate so many people but did not touch Daniel? The hungry lions were no match for the angels of God. The angels held back the lions. Divine protection was working for the servant of God. The angels of God are holding back whatever wants to destroy your life.

> Then the king arose very early in the morning, and went in haste unto the den of lions. And when he came to the den, he cried with a lamentable voice unto Daniel: and the king spake and said to Daniel, O DANIEL, SERVANT OF THE LIVING GOD, IS THY GOD, WHOM THOU SERVEST CONTINUALLY, ABLE TO DELIVER THEE FROM THE LIONS? Then said Daniel unto the king, O king, live for ever. My God hath sent his angel, and hath shut the lions' mouths, that they have not hurt me: forasmuch as before him innocency was found in me; and also before thee, O king, have I done no hurt.
>
> Then was the king exceeding glad for him, and commanded that they should take Daniel up out of the den. So Daniel was taken up out of the den, and no manner of hurt was found upon him, because he believed in his God.
>
> Daniel 6:19-23

4. **It is a great thing to serve the Lord because all those who hate you will be ashamed. By the power of God, all those who are incensed against you will be destroyed.**

In my short life, I have met people who seemed incensed against me. They wanted me to fall and they wanted me to be destroyed. When you are a servant of God, God will ensure that all those that are incensed against you will be ashamed and confounded. Many of those who laughed at me are no longer able to laugh so loud. May all your enemies be ashamed about what they said against you!

Thou whom I have taken from the ends of the earth, and called thee from the chief men thereof, and said unto thee, THOU ART MY SERVANT; I have chosen thee, and not cast thee away. Fear thou not; for I am with thee: be not dismayed; for I am thy God: I will strengthen thee; yea, I will help thee; yea, I will uphold thee with the right hand of my righteousness.

Behold, ALL THEY THAT WERE INCENSED AGAINST THEE SHALL BE ASHAMED AND CONFOUNDED: THEY SHALL BE AS NOTHING; and they that strive with thee shall perish. Thou shalt seek them, and shalt not find them, even them that contended with thee: they that war against thee shall be as nothing, and as a thing of nought. For I the Lord thy God will hold thy right hand, saying unto thee, Fear not; I will help thee. Fear not, thou worm Jacob, and ye men of Israel; I will help thee, saith the Lord, and thy redeemer, the Holy One of Israel.

Isaiah 41:9-14

CHAPTER 6

It is a Great Thing to Serve the Lord: *You Will Have Prosperity*

1. **It is a great thing to serve the Lord because when you are a servant of God, you will spend your days in prosperity.** Money is the reason why most people go to work. Money is what we need to live and survive in this world. We all know how money is earned. We have to go to school and we have to go to work. Through hard work, sweat and toil, you will be able to have all the money you need.

    But I know another factor that contributes greatly to your prosperity; the reality of being a servant of God. It is a great thing to serve the Lord because when you are a servant of God you will spend your days in prosperity and your years in pleasure. Prosperity is a clear promise to all servants of God. Expect to prosper when you serve God. Expect God to make you rich as you serve Him. Whatever job you do, know that serving God is key to your eventual prosperity.

    If they obey and serve him, THEY SHALL SPEND THEIR DAYS IN PROSPERITY, and their years

in pleasures. But if they obey not, they shall perish by the sword, and they shall die without knowledge.

Job 36:11-12

2.   **It is a great thing to serve the Lord because when you are a servant of God, God takes pleasure in your prosperity.** God actually enjoys giving you money because you are His servant. Do you believe the bible or not? It is time for you to accept the truth about prosperity. God likes it when His servants are rich, wealthy and prosperous. He takes pleasure in their prosperity. He has fun making his servants rich and directing money to them. He has pleasure in the prosperity of His servant.

Let them shout for joy, and be glad, that favour my righteous cause: yea, let them say continually, Let the LORD be magnified, WHICH HATH PLEASURE IN THE PROSPERITY OF HIS SERVANT.

Psalms 35:27

3.   **It is a great thing to serve the Lord because when you are a servant of God, you will enjoy overflowing abundance.**

And saw two ships standing by the lake: but the fishermen were gone out of them, and were washing their nets. And he entered into one of the ships, which was Simon's, and prayed him that he would thrust out a little from the land. And he sat down, and taught the people out of the ship. Now when he had left speaking, he said unto Simon, Launch out into the deep, and let down your nets for a draught. And Simon answering said unto him, Master, we have toiled all the night, and have taken nothing: nevertheless at thy word I will let down the net. And when they had this done, they inclosed a great multitude of fishes: and their net brake.

Luke 5:2-6

Peter was a fisherman and served his own interests. For a few moments, he served the interests of Jesus when he allowed Him to use his boat. Being God's servant and serving the interests of Jesus Christ brought a multiplied abundance far beyond any human effort. I would encourage every church worker and every businessman to believe the word of God and to learn from the testimonies of those who lived in the time of Jesus and had the privilege of obeying His instructions. God multiplies things under your hand because you help His purpose and serve His interests. Expect multiplied abundance because you are a servant of God!

4. **It is a great thing to serve the Lord because when you are a servant of God, He will deliver you from embarrassment.** Obeying the word of God and becoming servants of God will lead to abundance all the time. The embarrassing wine shortage at the wedding feast was cut short by the miracle that Jesus performed. The key to that miracle was obedience to the words of Jesus. Jesus' mother warned the attendants to obey Jesus. Similarly, when you obey the words of Jesus, "Seek ye first the kingdom of God and his righteousness", you become a servant of God and invoke super abundance over your life. Whatever is a source of embarrassment to you is cut off by the power of God at work in your life! Your life as a servant of God invokes the miracle of super abundance right now!

And the third day there was a marriage in Cana of Galilee; and the mother of Jesus was there: And both Jesus was called, and his disciples, to the marriage.

And when they wanted wine, the mother of Jesus saith unto him, They have no wine. Jesus saith unto her, Woman, what have I to do with thee? mine hour is not yet come. His mother saith unto the servants, WHATSOEVER HE SAITH UNTO YOU, DO IT. And there were set there six waterpots of stone, after the manner of the purifying of the Jews, containing two or three firkins apiece.

Jesus saith unto them, Fill the waterpots with water. And they filled them up to the brim. And he saith unto them, Draw out now, and bear unto the governor of the feast. And they bare it.

When the ruler of the feast had tasted the water that was made wine, and knew not whence it was:(but the servants which drew the water knew;) the governor of the feast called the bridegroom, And saith unto him, Every man at the beginning doth set forth good wine; and when men have well drunk, then that which is worse: but thou hast kept the good wine until now.

John 2:1-10

5. **It is a great thing to serve the Lord because when you are a servant of God, you shall never lack food.** Being a servant of God is simply obeying what God says. Obeying the word of God will result in you having enough food to eat for the rest of your life. You may not realize how much of a blessing it is till you know about millions of people who struggle to have enough food to eat every day. Provision of food is an important miracle for your life. When the disciples obeyed the instructions of Jesus to arrange the people in fifties, the miracle began to happen practically. As you begin to obey God practically and become His servant, you will see abundance and a provision like you never imagined!

And when the day began to wear away, then came the twelve, and said unto him, Send the multitude away, that they may go into the towns and country round about, and lodge, and get victuals: for we are here in a desert place. But he said unto them, Give ye them to eat. And they said, We have no more but five loaves and two fishes; except we should go and buy meat for all this people. For they were about five thousand men. And he said to his disciples, MAKE THEM SIT DOWN BY FIFTIES IN A COMPANY.

And they did so, and made them all sit down. Then he took the five loaves and the two fishes, and looking up to heaven, he blessed them, and brake, and gave to the disciples to set before the multitude.

And they did eat, and were all filled: and there was taken up of fragments that remained to them twelve baskets.

Luke 9:12-17

6.   **It is a great thing to serve the Lord because when you are a servant of God, you will receive lands and houses.**   God will give you a hundred fold of lands, houses and relationships in this life because of what you left for Him.   This scripture is either true or not true. Jesus Christ distinguishes between rewards on earth and rewards in heaven.   He promises rewards in this time for those who have left everything for His sake.   Expect to receive lands, houses, brethren and many other things because you serve God.

Then Peter began to say unto him, lo, we have left all, and have followed thee.

And Jesus answered and said, Verily I say unto you, There is no man that hath left house, or brethren, or sisters, or father, or mother, or wife, or children, or lands, for my sake, and the gospel's, But HE SHALL RECEIVE AN HUNDREDFOLD NOW IN THIS TIME, HOUSES, AND BRETHREN, and sisters, and mothers, and children, AND LANDS, with persecutions; and in the world to come eternal life. But many that are first shall be last; and the last first.

Mark 10:28-31

CHAPTER 7

It is a Great Thing to Serve the Lord:
You Will Serve and He Will Bless

1.   It is a great thing to serve the Lord because *YOU SHALL SERVE AND HE SHALL BLESS YOUR BREAD AND YOUR WATER.*

God gives diverse blessings to those who serve Him. The blessing on your bread and water results in sickness being taken away from you. God heals those who serve Him. God blesses them with healing. Expect to be healed because you are His servant. Your healing is an important blessing for serving the Lord. The contract is clear; you shall serve and He shall bless!

AND YE SHALL SERVE THE LORD YOUR GOD, AND HE SHALL BLESS thy bread, and thy water; and I will take sickness away from the midst of thee. There shall nothing cast their young, nor be barren, in thy land: the number of thy days I will fulfil.

Exodus 23:25-26

Serving God is a blessing for you. "You shall serve the Lord your God, and He shall bless".

I want you to remember this phrase:

And YE SHALL SERVE the Lord your God, and HE SHALL BLESS…!

And YE SHALL SERVE the Lord your God, and HE SHALL BLESS…!

And YE SHALL SERVE the Lord your God, and HE SHALL BLESS…!

And YE SHALL SERVE the Lord your God, and HE SHALL BLESS…!

And YE SHALL SERVE the Lord your God, and HE SHALL BLESS …!

And YE SHALL SERVE the Lord your God, and HE SHALL BLESS…!

And YE SHALL SERVE the Lord your God, and HE SHALL BLESS…!

To be called to serve God is to be called for a blessing. Stop thinking about what you can do for God. There is nothing that you can do for Him. Lift up your eyes and see the blessings that await those who serve the living God. God actually likes it when people expect blessings because they serve Him.

2.   **It is a great thing to serve the Lord because** *YOU SHALL SERVE AND HE SHALL BLESS: THERE WILL BE NO BARRENNESS AMONGST YOU.*

And YE SHALL SERVE THE LORD YOUR GOD, AND HE SHALL BLESS thy bread, and thy water; and I will take sickness away from the midst of thee. THERE SHALL NOTHING CAST THEIR YOUNG, NOR BE BARREN, in thy land: the number of thy days I will fulfil.

Exodus 23:25-26

Expect to have no barrenness in your midst. The blessing of having children is released abundantly in your life because you are His servant. Whatever causes barrenness in your life is destroyed today in the name of Jesus! When you pray, call on God and expect a miracle because you are a servant of God. God is with you and He will answer all your prayers. This is one of the divine blessings for serving the Lord.

I want you to remember this phrase:

And YE SHALL SERVE the Lord your God, and HE SHALL BLESS...!

And YE SHALL SERVE the Lord your God, and HE SHALL BLESS...!

And YE SHALL SERVE the Lord your God, and HE SHALL BLESS...!

And YE SHALL SERVE the Lord your God, and HE SHALL BLESS...!

And YE SHALL SERVE the Lord your God, and HE SHALL BLESS ...!

And YE SHALL SERVE the Lord your God, and HE SHALL BLESS...!

And YE SHALL SERVE the Lord your God, and HE SHALL BLESS...!

3.   **It is a great thing to serve the Lord because *YOU SHALL SERVE AND HE SHALL BLESS: YOU WILL LIVE LONG.***

And YE SHALL SERVE THE LORD YOUR GOD, AND HE SHALL BLESS thy bread, and thy water; and I will take sickness away from the midst of thee. There shall nothing cast their young, nor be barren, in thy land: THE NUMBER OF THY DAYS I WILL FULFIL.

Exodus 23:25-26

41

You are going to serve the Lord and He is going to bless you with long life. Do not expect to die anytime soon. You will live to between eighty and one hundred and twenty years. You will be strong and healthy throughout your life. You will never be on admission in the hospital and you will never be put on a drip. God will take care of you because you are His servant. He will cause you to fulfil the dream of long life. Even though there are many evil things that are cutting men's lives short, your life will be spared. Being a servant of God is no small thing. Remember:

And YE SHALL SERVE the Lord your God, and HE SHALL BLESS...!

And YE SHALL SERVE the Lord your God, and HE SHALL BLESS...!

And YE SHALL SERVE the Lord your God, and HE SHALL BLESS...!

And YE SHALL SERVE the Lord your God, and HE SHALL BLESS...!

4.   **It is a great thing to serve the Lord because** *YOU SHALL SERVE AND HE SHALL BLESS: THE BLESSING OF THE LORD WILL CAUSE YOU TO BECOME A BLESSING TO OTHERS.*

Now the Lord had said unto Abram, Get thee out of thy country, and from thy kindred, and from thy father's house, unto a land that I will shew thee: And I will make of thee a great nation, and I will bless thee, and make thy name great; AND THOU SHALT BE A BLESSING: And I will bless them that bless thee, and curse him that curseth thee: and in thee shall all families of the earth be blessed.

Genesis 12:1-3

You shall serve and He shall bless! As Abraham served God, God blessed him. God blessed him so much that he became a blessing. Abraham, the servant of God, became a blessing!

The greatest benefit of being blessed is to become a blessing. You are in a far better position in society if you are able to give a car to someone. Receiving a car is a great blessing. But being able to give a car is an even greater blessing! To receive a house is indeed a blessing. If you are ever able to give someone a house, you must indeed be a really blessed person. Only blessed people are able to give. God is changing your situation! Instead of opening your mouth wide like a newly born sparrow to only receive, God is turning things around. You are becoming a giver by the blessings of the Lord. If you do not have much, you simply cannot give.

5.   **It is a great thing to serve the Lord because *YOU SHALL SERVE AND HE SHALL BLESS: BLESSINGS WILL COME ON YOU AND OVERTAKE YOU.***

And it shall come to pass, if THOU SHALT HEARKEN DILIGENTLY UNTO THE VOICE OF THE LORD THY GOD, to observe and to do all his commandments which I command thee this day, that the Lord thy GOD WILL SET THEE ON HIGH ABOVE ALL NATIONS OF THE EARTH:

And all these blessings shall come on thee, and overtake thee, if thou shalt hearken unto the voice of the Lord thy God.

Deuteronomy 28:1-2

You shall serve the Lord and He shall bless. As you obey His words and become His servant, expect many blessings to be upon you. He will set you on high! He will promote you! You will be above all your colleagues and contemporaries, just because you are a servant of God.

So many blessings are determined for God's servants who are resolute about obeying His voice and serving Him. What an honour it is to be a servant of God! You will be lifted on high above all your colleagues. Divine promotion is coming your way because you are a servant of God. Kings shall come to your rising because you are a servant of God.

CHAPTER 8

It Is a Great Thing to Serve the Lord: *It is Not in Vain*

Therefore, my beloved brethren, be ye stedfast, unmoveable, always abounding in the work of the Lord, forasmuch as ye know that YOUR LABOUR IS NOT IN VAIN in the Lord.

1 Corinthians 15:58

Working for God is not in vain. Everything else is in vain! Every other job on this earth is in vain. It is only being a servant of God that is not in vain. It is not in vain because the results and rewards are spiritual and eternal. In this chapter, you will learn all the wonderful spiritual benefits of being a servant of God. It is indeed a great thing to serve the Lord. When you are a servant of the Lord, you have many spiritual and eternal blessings.

The list of spiritual blessings in this chapter is just too amazing. Please believe in all the blessings that come to the servant of God. There are things in the bible we are expected to just believe. Do not try too hard to understand how and why all these blessings will come upon you because you are a servant of God. Have faith in God and you will experience all these prophecies practically.

1. **It is a great thing to serve the Lord because your sins are blotted out.** You and I are so sinful. We commit so many mistakes and there is no good reason for God to use any of us. It is necessary that your sins be blotted out. Indeed, your sins are blotted out just because you have become a servant of God. Years ago, I discovered that one of my father's employees was a thief. Then I discovered that my father already knew that he was a thief. Initially, I was puzzled and wondered why my father would not get rid of this servant who was a well-known pilferer. I realised that my father had ignored (blotted out) his servant's sins. He simply took no notice of all the stealing that was going on. He seemed to value this servant so much that he never sacked him. It is amazing how many transgressions and sins of a servant will be blotted out by a master.

Remember these, O Jacob and Israel; for thou art my servant: I have formed thee; THOU ART MY SERVANT: O Israel, thou shalt not be forgotten of me. I HAVE BLOTTED

OUT, as a thick cloud, THY TRANSGRESSIONS, and, as a cloud, thy sins: return unto me; for I have redeemed thee.

Isaiah 44:21-22

2. **It is a great thing to serve the Lord because God's words are confirmed in your life.** God will honour the words that you speak. He will ensure that your prophecies do not fall to the ground.

Thus saith the Lord, thy redeemer, and he that formed thee from the womb, I AM THE LORD that maketh all things; that stretcheth forth the heavens alone; that spreadeth abroad the earth by myself ....THAT CONFIRMETH THE WORD OF HIS SERVANT, and performeth the counsel of his messengers; that saith to Jerusalem, Thou shalt be inhabited; and to the cities of Judah, Ye shall be built, and I will raise up the decayed places thereof:

Isaiah 44:24, 26

3. **It is a great thing to serve the Lord because you will be used all over the world by God.** I have travelled all over the world as a servant of God. I would not have seen many of the places I have seen if I was not a servant of God. Being a servant of God has made me proclaim salvation to the ends of the earth. What an honour it is to be a servant of God!

And said unto me, THOU ART MY SERVANT, O ISRAEL, in whom I will be glorified. Then I said, I have laboured in vain, I have spent my strength for nought, and in vain: yet surely my judgment is with the Lord, and my work with my God. And now, saith the Lord that formed me FROM THE WOMB TO BE HIS SERVANT, to bring Jacob again to him, Though Israel be not gathered, yet shall I be glorious in the eyes of the Lord, and my God shall be my strength. And he said, It is a light thing that thou shouldest be my servant to raise up the tribes of Jacob, and to restore the preserved of Israel: I WILL ALSO GIVE THEE FOR

A LIGHT TO THE GENTILES, THAT THOU MAYEST
BE MY SALVATION UNTO THE END OF THE EARTH.

Isaiah 49:3-6

4.   **It is a great thing to serve the Lord because you will
     come near to God.**   God is a God who blesses those
     whom He has chosen to serve Him. To be called to work
     for God is a blessing. You cannot improve God in any
     way. You cannot make God look good or bad. You and
     I are nothing. We need God! God does not need us!
     The scripture above says, "Blessed is the man whom God
     chooses." When you are chosen by God, you are blessed.
     It is you who is blessed when you are chosen.

Blessed is THE MAN WHOM THOU CHOOSEST, and
causest to approach unto thee, that he may dwell in thy
courts: we shall be satisfied with the goodness of thy
house, even of thy holy temple.

Psalm 65:4

For, behold, those who are far from You will perish; You
hast destroyed all those who are unfaithful to You. BUT
AS FOR ME, THE NEARNESS OF GOD IS MY GOOD;
I have made the Lord GOD my refuge, that I may tell of
all Your works.

Psalms 73:27-28 (NASB)

5.   **It is a great thing to serve the Lord because God will
     honour you.**   There may be nothing in this life that will
     bring you honour except God. Serving God is the most
     honourable thing you could ever do. You will receive
     more honour in your life by being a servant of God.

If any man serve me, let him follow me; and where I am,
there shall also my servant be: IF ANY MAN SERVE ME,
HIM WILL MY FATHER HONOUR.

John 12:26

6. **It is a great thing to serve the Lord because God will spare you.**

   And they shall be mine, saith the Lord of hosts, in that day when I make up my jewels; AND I WILL SPARE THEM, AS A MAN SPARETH HIS OWN SON THAT SERVETH HIM. Then shall ye return, and discern between the righteous and the wicked, between him that serveth God and him that serveth him not.

   Malachi 3:17-18

7. **It is a great thing to serve the Lord because you will know the secrets of God.** You do not tell your secrets to everyone. Why do you think God would reveal His secrets to everyone? When you become a servant, He will tell you His secrets and tell you about the future.

   Surely the Lord God will do nothing, but HE REVEALETH HIS SECRET UNTO HIS SERVANTS THE PROPHETS.

   Amos 3:7

CHAPTER 9

It Is a Great Thing to Serve the Lord: *You Will Receive Temple Blessings*

The people who serve God in His temple night and day have many benefits. In the book of Revelation, we see the secret of what it really means to have such a position and to have such a job.

> **Therefore are they before the throne of God, and SERVE HIM DAY AND NIGHT IN HIS TEMPLE: and he that sitteth on the throne shall dwell among them. They shall hunger no more, neither thirst any more; neither shall the sun light on them, nor any heat. For the Lamb which is in the midst of the throne shall feed them, and shall lead them unto living fountains of waters: and God shall wipe away all tears from their eyes.**
>
> **Revelation 7:15-17**

In the book of Revelation, we have a wonderful picture of people serving in the temple of God. This vision shows us what it really means to serve the Lord. Read it for yourself and be amazed at the benefits of being a servant of the Lord.

One of the greatest blessings of serving God is the blessing of being looked after by the Lord Himself. Serving God totally, in His house, results in your being totally looked after by the Lamb.

The great blessing of serving the Lord cannot be compared with any other kind of service to any organization or person.

David said, "One thing have I desired of the Lord, that will I seek after; that I may dwell in the house of the Lord all the days of my life, to behold the beauty of the Lord, and to enquire in his temple" (Psalm 27:4). You do not have to get to heaven to serve in His temple. You can equally serve Him right now. Expect these eight wonderful rewards when you serve the Lord in His temple.

Eight Benefits of Serving in the Temple

1. *No more hunger.* You will never lack food till you die.

   They shall HUNGER NO MORE, neither thirst any more; neither shall the sun light on them, nor any heat.

   Revelation 7:16

2. *No more thirst.* You will never be thirsty or uncomfortable.

   They shall hunger no more, NEITHER THIRST ANY MORE; neither shall the sun light on them, nor any heat.

   Revelation 7:16

3. *Protection from the sun.* You will not be destroyed by the sunshine. You will have a house and a car to protect you from the direct sunshine. I once had a vision of three lay pastors, labouring in the sun and heat. The Holy Spirit told me that these pastors were labouring in the secular world, when they should be in the house of God. I called each one of them and invited them to come over into the temple and serve God Himself. Unfortunately, one

of them opted to continue in the sun and heat where he remains until this day.

They shall hunger no more, neither thirst any more; NEITHER SHALL THE SUN LIGHT ON THEM, nor any heat.

Revelation 7:16

4.   *Protection from heat.* You will no longer sweat in the day or in the night. Expect God to make you comfortable as you serve Him. Expect to have air conditioners cooling your environment all the time. God will give you enough money to buy a generator, a fan and an air conditioner.

They shall hunger no more, neither thirst any more; neither shall the sun light on them, NOR ANY HEAT.

Revelation 7:16

5.   *Being fed by the Lord.* Expect God to feed you Himself. You will be pampered and loved because you served the Lord. God could have simply removed hunger from your life. But He decided to feed you Himself. This shows the extent to which God wants to rub you down and pamper you.

For THE LAMB which is in the midst of the throne SHALL FEED THEM, and shall lead them unto living fountains of waters: and God shall wipe away all tears from their eyes.

Revelation 7:17

6.   *Being led by the Lord to living fountains.* You will be brought to living fountains of water. All over the world, people go to beaches to experience the fun and thrill of the oceans. Living water creates such an exhilarating feeling. You have been promised an everlasting holiday with living fountains of waters spraying all over you just because you are serving the Lord. I feel sorry for people who think that serving the Lord is boring.

For THE LAMB which is in the midst of the throne shall feed them, and SHALL LEAD THEM UNTO LIVING FOUNTAINS of waters: and God shall wipe away all tears from their eyes.

Revelation 7:17

7.   *The removal of sorrows and tears.*   Life on this earth is punctuated by tears, grief and sorrow. Serving in His temple is marked by the notable absence of sorrowful tears. You will cry no more when you serve the Lord.

For the Lamb which is in the midst of the throne shall feed them, and shall lead them unto living fountains of waters: and GOD SHALL WIPE AWAY ALL TEARS FROM THEIR EYES.

Revelation 7:17

8.   *You will become a shining star in eternity.*   God makes you shine when you win souls for Him. You will shine forever in eternity because you served the Lord.

And they that be wise shall shine as the brightness of the firmament; and they that turn many to righteousness as the stars for ever and ever.

Daniel 12:3

CHAPTER 10

It Is A Great Thing to Serve the Lord: *You Will Not Serve the Enemy*

Serving God is very important because, whatever the case, you will definitely serve something or someone. Who will you serve? Who will you work for? What will govern your life? What will make you wake up early in the morning and go to work? What will you die for? What will you spend your life's energy and zeal on? What will make you undertake many journeys? What will you bow to? What will you yield to? Who will you serve? What will you serve?

You will definitely serve someone! You will definitely serve something. You will work for someone, even if it is yourself. When God offers you a chance to serve Him, He is offering you a chance to escape serving your enemy. There are many different kinds of enemies you could serve. None of these enemies is worth serving. It is always better to serve the Lord. God laughs from heaven as men choose to serve wood and stone, rather than serve Him, the Creator. What a shame it is for man to bow down and serve stone and wood rather than serve the Maker of all these.

Worst of all is the possibility that you could be serving satan instead of serving God. Satan is such a wicked master.

Anytime demons are in control they inflict harsh, cruel measures on those they exert power over. It is sad to see the cruel measures meted out by satan.

It is time to serve the Lord! It is time to distance yourself from everything demonic. Choose God! By choosing God you are choosing not to serve wood, stones or even Pharaoh.

1. **If you do not serve the Lord, you will be handed over to serve your enemies.**

   BECAUSE THOU SERVEDST NOT THE LORD THY GOD with joyfulness, and with gladness of heart, for the abundance of all things;

   THEREFORE SHALT THOU SERVE THINE ENEMIES WHICH THE LORD SHALL SEND AGAINST THEE, IN HUNGER, AND IN THIRST, AND IN NAKEDNESS, AND IN WANT OF ALL THINGS: and he shall put a yoke of iron upon thy neck, until he have destroyed thee.

   Deuteronomy 28:47-48

   God wants to enjoy you. God wants to be happy with you and wants to enjoy you serving Him. If you do not enjoy God, He will hand you over to serve the alternative. If you do not want to serve God, the other option is to serve His enemy.

   Many people who have rejected Christianity are being forced to accept an alternative religion with all its implications. God's punishment for His people who do not want to serve Him is to serve the enemy in hunger, in thirst and in the want of all things. There are people who should be in the ministry, serving God all their lives. Today, many such people are working for the enemy day and night, building financial kingdoms for unbelievers. They get peanuts for all their hard work and basically advance the agenda of demonized men. Satan rejoices as God's best treasures are locked down in Pharaoh's pyramids, building monuments to the glory of the enemy. You must remember that the wealth of the world lies in the hands of a few powerful people who mostly hate God.

2. **If you do not serve the Lord, you will be handed over to serve other gods; idols.**

    And the Lord shall scatter thee among all people, from the one end of the earth even unto the other; and there THOU SHALT SERVE OTHER GODS, which neither thou nor thy fathers have known, even wood and stone.

    Deuteronomy 28:64

    You may be forced to serve other gods because you did not serve the Lord. Most of the people who have rejected Christianity have turned to some other kind of religion. Many other religions have flourished in the places where Christianity has been rejected. I was once in a city which was once a beautiful example of powerful Christian influence. Right in the centre of the city I saw a statue dedicated to witchcraft. I marvelled at how the Christian city could turn away and move completely into darkness. Indeed, if you will not serve the living God, you will be forced to serve other gods.

3. **If you do not serve the Lord, you will be handed over to serve wood and stone.**

    When you do not choose to serve the Lord, you will serve wood and stone. You will build with wood and stone and end up dying for the wood and the stone!

    The Lord shall bring thee, and thy king which thou shalt set over thee, unto a nation which neither thou nor thy fathers have known; and there shalt THOU SERVE OTHER GODS, WOOD AND STONE.

    And thou shalt become an astonishment, a proverb, and a byword, among all nations whither the Lord shall lead thee.

    Deuteronomy 28:36-37

4.   **If you do not serve the Lord, you will become a proverb, a byword and a wonder.**

Moreover all these curses shall come upon thee, and shall pursue thee, and overtake thee, till thou be destroyed; because thou hearkenedst not unto the voice of the Lord thy God, to keep his commandments and his statutes which he commanded thee: And THEY SHALL BE UPON THEE FOR A SIGN AND FOR A WONDER, and upon thy seed for ever.

Deuteronomy 28:45-46

Because you did not serve the Lord, you become a proverb, a sign and a wonder.   God looks at you in sadness as men mock you and use you as a bad example for everything.   You are a sign, a wonder and an amazement just because you did not choose to serve the Lord.   From now you must choose to serve God.

5.   **If you do not serve the Lord, you will serve Pharaoh and he will give you very hard labour.**

And Pharaoh commanded the same day the taskmasters of the people, and their officers, saying, Ye shall no more give the people straw to make brick, as heretofore: let them go and gather straw for themselves. And the tale of the bricks, which they did make heretofore, ye shall lay upon them; ye shall not diminish ought thereof: for they be idle; therefore they cry, saying, Let us go and sacrifice to our God. LET THERE MORE WORK BE LAID UPON THE MEN, THAT THEY MAY LABOUR THEREIN;...

Exodus 5:6-9

To serve Pharaoh is to serve satan.   Pharaoh is a "type" of satan.   Moses is a "type" of Christ.   Moses was sent to deliver the people of God from the great bondage of satan (Pharaoh). All the service of the children of Israel under the hand of

Pharaoh typifies what it is like to serve satan in the world today. People are prevented from serving God by Pharaoh who will hardly let them go.

What happened to the children of Israel was just an example to those of us who have been saved through Christ. Moses was a type of Christ who saved the Israelites. Pharaoh was a type of satan who does not want people to serve God. Pharaoh was continually told: "Let my people go, that they may serve me." Pharaoh did not want the people of God to go. He did not want them to serve God. Today, there are many jobs that do not allow you to serve God. There are many nations that do not allow you to serve God. There are many circumstances that do not allow you to serve God.

As Pharaoh prevented the Israelites from serving God, your jobs, your bosses, your superiors may be preventing you from serving God. The alternative to serving the Lord with gladness is to serve your enemies.

6.   **If you do not serve the Lord, you will serve Pharaoh and your life will be used to build the cities of this world.**

You could have been building the cities of the Lord but you chose to build the cities of this world under Pharaoh's leadership. Instead of serving the Lord, you will just contribute to the building of great cities on planet earth. Is that all you want to accomplish with your life – to build the cities of London, Accra, Lagos, Paris and New York? I want to be involved in building the kingdom of God.

Therefore they did set over them taskmasters to afflict them with their burdens. And THEY BUILT FOR PHARAOH TREASURE CITIES, PITHOM AND RAAMSES.

Exodus 1:11

7.   **If you do not serve the Lord, you will serve Pharaoh and he will give you wicked men to be over you.**

To serve Pharaoh is to serve evil men and murderers. The Egyptians were murderers because they had given instructions to murder all Hebrew children.

And the king of Egypt spake to the Hebrew midwives, of which the name of the one was Shiphrah, and the name of the other Puah:

And he said, When ye do the office of a midwife to the Hebrew women, and see them upon the stools; IF IT BE A SON, THEN YE SHALL KILL HIM: but if it be a daughter, then she shall live.

But the midwives feared God, and did not as the king of Egypt commanded them, but saved the men children alive.

                                        Exodus 1:15-17

Remember: Pharaoh will hardly let anyone go! You must fight to be free! You must fight to serve God! Pharaoh will not let you go easily! It will not be easy to break out and serve the Lord.

And it came to pass, when PHARAOH WOULD HARDLY LET US GO, that the Lord slew all the firstborn in the land of Egypt, both the firstborn of man, and the firstborn of beast: therefore I sacrifice to the Lord all that openeth the matrix, being males; but all the firstborn of my children I redeem.

                                        Exodus 13:15

8.   **If you do not serve the Lord, you will serve Pharaoh and he will prevent you from going very far with God.**

It is time to go all out. We are going as far as God wants us to go. Do not let anyone tell you how far you must go with God.

And Moses said, It is not meet so to do; for we shall sacrifice the abomination of the Egyptians to the Lord

our God: lo, shall we sacrifice the abomination of the Egyptians before their eyes, and will they not stone us? We will go three days' journey into the wilderness, and sacrifice to the Lord our God, as he shall command us. And Pharaoh said, I will let you go, that ye may sacrifice to the Lord your God in the wilderness; only YE SHALL NOT GO VERY FAR AWAY: intreat for me.

Exodus 8:26-28

9.   **If you do not serve the Lord, you will serve Pharaoh and he will steal all your flocks and herds.**

Most people are disappointed at the end of their lives. They have served Pharaoh and it has amounted to nothing.

And Moses said, We will go with our young and with our old, with our sons and with our daughters, WITH OUR FLOCKS AND WITH OUR HERDS will we go; for we must hold a feast unto the Lord.

Exodus 10:9

10.   **If you do not serve the Lord, you will serve Pharaoh and he will take over your family.**

Satan would love to have your family if he cannot have you. By serving the Lord, you deliver your family from wickedness and evil. Many children are saved just because their parents serve God. One of the blessings of serving God is for your children to be saved. Satan desperately wants your seed but God has a plan for them. Fight to be free from Pharaoh! You are fighting for your children!

And Moses said, WE WILL GO WITH OUR YOUNG AND WITH OUR OLD, with OUR SONS and with OUR DAUGHTERS, with our flocks and with our herds will we go; for we must hold a feast unto the Lord.

Exodus 10:9

It Is A Great Thing to Serve the Lord: *The Prophetic Heritage of A Servant of God*

... This is the HERITAGE of the servants of the LORD...

Isaiah 54:17

T he servant of the Lord has a great heritage. He is destined for greatness in a supernatural way.

Most Christians do not read the book of Isaiah very much. Perhaps they know a couple of scriptures from Isaiah, but most of us hardly understand much of it. However, it is the book most quoted from by Jesus and it is also the book that describes Jesus' ministry in amazing detail. It is also the book that describes the heritage of a servant of God in much detail. It is very important for us to glean the revelation God has for us in there. I believe you will be mightily blessed by this wonderful prophet!

There are twelve specific prophecies about God's servants in the book of Isaiah. The prophet spoke clearly about the heritage of anyone called the servant of the Lord. These prophecies are self-explanatory and reveal God's mind towards his servants. Indeed, there is no higher privilege than to be called God's servant.

Do not let anyone take you away from the great honour of being a servant of God. The heritage of a servant of God is too good to be true! I want to be a servant of God! I want to serve Him even more than I have done so far! I wish I could live longer just to serve Him some more! What a blessing it is to be called a servant of God!

I want you to read the prophecies of Isaiah concerning a servant of God over and over. As you do, believe in the incredible blessings that are prophesied about your heritage as a servant of God.

Remember, these are not blessings for just anyone. They are blessings for a servant of God! They are not spoken just for ordinary people but for those who are called "servants of God".

Please note that each time the prophet began to declare the blessings and heritage of God's servants, he said many things. So many amazing things! Some hard to believe!

Because of the multitude of varied statements Isaiah made about God's servants, I have decided not to comment about them but just to reproduce them as they are. From now, you will always know where to find the twelve prophecies about the servant of God. As you meditate on these prophecies, they will soak into your spirit. You will practically experience all the things prophesied about a servant of God! These prophecies describe the heritage of the servants of God.

Twelve Prophecies about the Servant of God

1. The first prophetic heritage of a servant of God.

BUT THOU, ISRAEL, ART MY SERVANT, Jacob whom I have chosen, the seed of Abraham my friend. Thou whom I have taken from the ends of the earth, and called thee from the chief men thereof, and said unto thee, THOU ART MY SERVANT; I have chosen thee, and not cast thee away. Fear thou not; for I AM WITH THEE: be not dismayed; for I AM THY GOD: I WILL STRENGTHEN THEE; yea, I WILL HELP THEE; yea, I WILL UPHOLD THEE with the right hand of my righteousness.

Behold, ALL THEY THAT WERE INCENSED AGAINST THEE SHALL BE ASHAMED AND CONFOUNDED: THEY SHALL BE AS NOTHING; and they that strive with thee shall perish. Thou shalt seek them, and shalt not find them, even them that contended with thee: THEY THAT WAR AGAINST THEE SHALL BE AS NOTHING, and as a thing of nought. For I the Lord thy God WILL HOLD THY RIGHT HAND, saying unto thee, Fear not; I will help thee. Fear not, thou worm Jacob, and ye men of Israel; I will help thee, saith the Lord, and thy redeemer, the Holy One of Israel. Behold, I WILL MAKE THEE A NEW SHARP THRESHING INSTRUMENT having teeth: thou shalt thresh the mountains, and beat them small, and shalt make the hills as chaff. Thou shalt fan them, and the wind shall carry them away, and the whirlwind shall scatter them: and THOU SHALT REJOICE IN THE LORD, and shalt glory in the Holy One of Israel.

Isaiah 41:8-16

2.   The second prophetic heritage of a servant of God.

BEHOLD MY SERVANT, whom I uphold; mine elect, in whom my soul delighteth; I HAVE PUT MY SPIRIT UPON HIM: he shall bring forth judgment to the Gentiles. He shall not cry, nor lift up, nor cause his voice to be heard in the street. A bruised reed shall he not break, and the smoking flax shall he not quench: he shall bring forth judgment unto truth. HE SHALL NOT FAIL NOR BE DISCOURAGED, till he have set judgment in the earth: and the isles shall wait for his law. Thus saith God the Lord, he that created the heavens, and stretched them out; he that spread forth the earth, and that which cometh out of it; he that giveth breath unto the people upon it, and spirit to them that walk therein: I THE LORD HAVE CALLED THEE IN RIGHTEOUSNESS, AND WILL HOLD THINE HAND, AND WILL KEEP THEE, AND GIVE THEE FOR A COVENANT OF THE PEOPLE, FOR A LIGHT OF THE GENTILES; TO OPEN THE BLIND EYES, TO BRING OUT THE PRISONERS FROM THE PRISON, AND THEM THAT SIT IN DARKNESS OUT OF THE PRISON HOUSE. I am the Lord: that is my name: and my glory will I not give to another, neither my praise to graven images. Behold, the former things are come to pass, and new things do I declare: before they spring forth I tell you of them.

Isaiah 42:1-9

3.   The third prophetic heritage of a servant of God.

But now thus saith the Lord that created thee, O Jacob, and he that formed thee, O Israel, Fear not: for I have redeemed thee, I have called thee by thy name; thou art mine. WHEN THOU PASSEST THROUGH THE WATERS, I WILL BE WITH THEE; AND THROUGH THE RIVERS,

THEY SHALL NOT OVERFLOW THEE: WHEN THOU WALKEST THROUGH THE FIRE, THOU SHALT NOT BE BURNED; neither shall the flame kindle upon thee. For I am the Lord thy God, the Holy One of Israel, thy Saviour: I gave Egypt for thy ransom, Ethiopia and Seba for thee.

Since thou wast precious in my sight, thou hast been honourable, and I HAVE LOVED THEE: THEREFORE WILL I GIVE MEN FOR THEE, AND PEOPLE FOR THY LIFE. Fear not: for I am with thee: I will bring thy seed from the east, and gather thee from the west; I WILL SAY TO THE NORTH, GIVE UP; AND TO THE SOUTH, KEEP NOT BACK: BRING MY SONS FROM FAR, AND MY DAUGHTERS FROM THE ENDS OF THE EARTH; Even every one that is called by my name: for I have created him for my glory, I have formed him; yea, I have made him. Bring forth the blind people that have eyes, and the deaf that have ears. Let all the nations be gathered together, and let the people be assembled: who among them can declare this, and shew us former things? let them bring forth their witnesses, that they may be justified: or let them hear, and say, It is truth. Ye are my witnesses, saith the Lord, and MY SERVANT WHOM I HAVE CHOSEN: that ye may know and believe me, and understand that I am he: before me there was no God formed, neither shall there be after me.

Isaiah 43:1-10

4.   The fourth prophetic heritage of a servant of God.

Yet now hear, O Jacob my servant; and Israel, whom I have chosen: Thus saith the Lord that made thee, and formed thee from the womb, which will help thee; FEAR NOT, O JACOB, MY SERVANT; AND THOU, JESURUN, WHOM I HAVE CHOSEN. For I WILL POUR WATER UPON HIM THAT IS THIRSTY, AND FLOODS UPON THE DRY GROUND: I WILL POUR MY SPIRIT UPON THY SEED, AND MY BLESSING UPON THINE

OFFSPRING: AND THEY SHALL SPRING UP AS AMONG THE GRASS, as willows by the water courses.

Isaiah 44:1-4

5.   The fifth prophetic heritage of the servant of God.

Remember these, O Jacob and Israel; for thou art my servant: I have formed thee; THOU ART MY SERVANT: O Israel, THOU SHALT NOT BE FORGOTTEN OF ME. I HAVE BLOTTED OUT, as a thick cloud, THY TRANSGRESSIONS, and, as a cloud, thy sins: return unto me; for I have redeemed thee. Sing, O ye heavens; for the Lord hath done it: shout, ye lower parts of the earth: break forth into singing, ye mountains, O forest, and every tree therein: for the Lord hath redeemed Jacob, and glorified himself in Israel. Thus saith the Lord, thy redeemer, and he that formed thee from the womb, I am the Lord that maketh all things; that stretcheth forth the heavens alone; that spreadeth abroad the earth by myself; That frustrateth the tokens of the liars, and maketh diviners mad; that turneth wise men backward, and maketh their knowledge foolish; THAT CONFIRMETH THE WORD OF HIS SERVANT, AND PERFORMETH THE COUNSEL OF HIS MESSENGERS; that saith to Jerusalem, Thou shalt be inhabited; and to the cities of Judah, Ye shall be built, and I will raise up the decayed places thereof: That saith to the deep, Be dry, and I will dry up thy rivers: THAT SAITH OF CYRUS, HE IS MY SHEPHERD, AND SHALL PERFORM ALL MY PLEASURE: EVEN SAYING TO JERUSALEM, THOU SHALT BE BUILT; AND TO THE TEMPLE, THY FOUNDATION SHALL BE LAID.

Isaiah 44:21-28

6.   The sixth prophetic heritage of the servant of the Lord.

Listen, O isles, unto me; and hearken, ye people, from far; The Lord hath called me from the womb; from the bowels of my mother hath he made mention of my name. And he

65

hath made my mouth like a sharp sword; in the shadow of his hand hath he hid me, and made me a polished shaft; in his quiver hath he hid me; And said unto me, THOU ART MY SERVANT, O Israel, in whom I will be glorified. Then I said, I have laboured in vain, I have spent my strength for nought, and in vain: yet surely my judgment is with the Lord, and my work with my God. And now, saith the Lord that formed me from the womb to be his servant, to bring Jacob again to him, Though Israel be not gathered, yet shall I be glorious in the eyes of the Lord, and my God shall be my strength. And he said, IT IS A LIGHT THING THAT THOU SHOULDEST BE MY SERVANT TO RAISE UP THE TRIBES OF JACOB, AND TO RESTORE THE PRESERVED OF ISRAEL: I WILL ALSO GIVE THEE FOR A LIGHT TO THE GENTILES, THAT THOU MAYEST BE MY SALVATION UNTO THE END OF THE EARTH. Thus saith the Lord, the Redeemer of Israel, and his Holy One, to him whom man despiseth, to him whom the nation abhorreth, to a servant of rulers, Kings shall see and arise, princes also shall worship, because of the Lord that is faithful, and the Holy One of Israel, and he shall choose thee.

Thus saith the Lord, IN AN ACCEPTABLE TIME HAVE I HEARD THEE, AND IN A DAY OF SALVATION HAVE I HELPED THEE: AND I WILL PRESERVE THEE, AND GIVE THEE FOR A COVENANT OF THE PEOPLE, TO ESTABLISH THE EARTH, TO CAUSE TO INHERIT THE DESOLATE HERITAGES; That thou mayest say to the prisoners, Go forth; to them that are in darkness, Shew yourselves. They shall feed in the ways, and their pastures shall be in all high places. They shall not hunger nor thirst; neither shall the heat nor sun smite them: for he that hath mercy on them shall lead them, even by the springs of water shall he guide them. And I will make all my mountains a way, and my highways shall be exalted. Behold, these shall come from far: and, lo, these from the north and from the west; and these from the land of Sinim. Sing, O heavens; and be joyful, O earth; and break forth into singing, O mountains: for the Lord hath comforted his people, and will have mercy upon his afflicted.

Isaiah 49:1-13

7. The seventh prophetic heritage of the servant of the Lord.

Behold, MY SERVANT shall deal prudently, he SHALL BE EXALTED AND EXTOLLED, AND BE VERY HIGH. As many were astonied at thee; his visage was so marred more than any man, and his form more than the sons of men: So shall he sprinkle many nations; the kings shall shut their mouths at him: for that which had not been told them shall they see; and that which they had not heard shall they consider.

Isaiah 52:13-15

8. The eighth prophetic heritage of the servant of the Lord.

He shall see of the travail of his soul, and shall be satisfied: BY HIS KNOWLEDGE SHALL MY RIGHTEOUS SERVANT JUSTIFY MANY; For he shall bear their iniquities. Therefore will I divide him a portion with the great, and he shall divide the spoil with the strong; because he hath poured out his soul unto death: and he was numbered with the transgressors; and he bare the sin of many, and made intercession for the transgressors.

Isaiah 53:11-12

9. The ninth prophetic heritage of the servant of the Lord.

O thou afflicted, tossed with tempest, and not comforted, behold, I will lay thy stones with fair colours, and lay thy foundations with sapphires. And I will make thy windows of agates, and thy gates of carbuncles, and all thy borders of pleasant stones. And ALL THY CHILDREN SHALL BE

TAUGHT OF THE LORD; AND GREAT SHALL BE THE PEACE OF THY CHILDREN. IN RIGHTEOUSNESS SHALT THOU BE ESTABLISHED: THOU SHALT BE FAR FROM OPPRESSION; for thou shalt not fear: and from terror; for it shall not come near thee. Behold, they shall surely gather together, but not by me: whosoever shall gather together against thee shall fall for thy sake. Behold, I have created the smith that bloweth the coals in the fire, and that bringeth forth an instrument for his work; and I have created the waster to destroy. NO WEAPON THAT IS FORMED AGAINST THEE SHALL PROSPER; AND EVERY TONGUE THAT SHALL RISE AGAINST THEE IN JUDGMENT THOU SHALT CONDEMN. THIS IS THE HERITAGE OF THE SERVANTS OF THE LORD, AND THEIR RIGHTEOUSNESS IS OF ME, SAITH THE LORD.

Isaiah 54:11-17

10. The tenth prophetic heritage of the servant of the Lord.

Neither let the son of the stranger, that hath joined himself to the Lord, speak, saying, The Lord hath utterly separated me from his people: neither let the eunuch say, Behold, I am a dry tree. For thus saith the Lord unto the eunuchs that keep my sabbaths, and choose the things that please me, and take hold of my covenant; Even unto them will I give in mine house and within my walls a place and a name better than of sons and of daughters: I will give them an everlasting name, that shall not be cut off. ALSO THE SONS OF THE STRANGER, THAT JOIN THEMSELVES TO THE LORD, TO SERVE HIM, AND TO LOVE THE NAME OF THE LORD, TO BE HIS SERVANTS, EVERY ONE THAT KEEPETH THE SABBATH FROM POLLUTING IT, AND TAKETH HOLD OF MY COVENANT; EVEN THEM WILL I BRING TO MY HOLY MOUNTAIN, AND MAKE THEM JOYFUL IN MY HOUSE OF PRAYER: their burnt offerings and their sacrifices shall be accepted upon mine altar; for mine house shall be called an house of prayer for all people.

Isaiah 56:3-7

11. The eleventh prophetic heritage of servant of the Lord.

THUS SAITH THE LORD, AS THE NEW WINE IS FOUND IN THE CLUSTER, AND ONE SAITH, DESTROY IT NOT; FOR A BLESSING IS IN IT: SO WILL I DO FOR MY SERVANTS' SAKES, THAT I MAY NOT DESTROY THEM ALL. And I will bring forth a seed out of Jacob, and out of Judah an inheritor of my mountains: and mine elect shall inherit it, and my servants shall dwell there. And Sharon shall be a fold of flocks, and the valley of Achor a place for the herds to lie down in, for my people that have sought me. But ye are they that forsake the Lord, that forget my holy mountain, that prepare a table for that troop, and that furnish the drink offering unto that number. Therefore will I number you to the sword, and ye shall all bow down to the slaughter: because when I called, ye did not answer; when I spake, ye did not hear; but did evil before mine eyes, and did choose that wherein I delighted not. Therefore thus saith the Lord God, BEHOLD, MY SERVANTS SHALL EAT, BUT YE SHALL BE HUNGRY: BEHOLD, MY SERVANTS SHALL DRINK, BUT YE SHALL BE THIRSTY: BEHOLD, MY SERVANTS SHALL REJOICE, BUT YE SHALL BE ASHAMED: BEHOLD, MY SERVANTS SHALL SING FOR JOY OF HEART, BUT YE SHALL CRY FOR SORROW OF HEART, AND SHALL HOWL FOR VEXATION OF SPIRIT. AND YE SHALL LEAVE YOUR NAME FOR A CURSE UNTO MY CHOSEN: FOR THE LORD GOD SHALL SLAY THEE, AND CALL HIS SERVANTS BY ANOTHER NAME:

Isaiah 65:8-15

12. The twelfth prophetic heritage of the servants of the Lord.

Rejoice ye with Jerusalem, and be glad with her, all ye that love her: rejoice for joy with her, all ye that mourn for her: THAT YE MAY SUCK, AND BE SATISFIED WITH THE BREASTS OF HER CONSOLATIONS; THAT YE MAY MILK OUT, AND BE DELIGHTED WITH THE ABUNDANCE OF HER GLORY. FOR THUS SAITH THE LORD, BEHOLD, I WILL EXTEND PEACE TO HER LIKE A RIVER, AND THE GLORY OF THE GENTILES LIKE A FLOWING STREAM: THEN SHALL YE SUCK, YE SHALL BE BORNE UPON HER SIDES, AND BE DANDLED UPON HER KNEES. As one whom his mother comforteth, so will I comfort you; and ye shall be comforted in Jerusalem. And when ye see this, your heart shall rejoice, and your bones shall flourish like an herb: and THE HAND OF THE LORD SHALL BE KNOWN TOWARD HIS SERVANTS, and his indignation toward his enemies.

Isaiah 66:10-14

May you always be a SERVANT of the Lord!

... This is the HERITAGE of the servants of the LORD...

Isaiah 54:17

THE END